Steve Light is one of the truly great poets of our time. We would be hard pressed to find a voice in which the dialogue with philosophy that is always latent in poetry (perhaps its very essence even) to be so succinctly and essentially crafted. But an interlocution fashioned precisely *as poetry*, and that at its fullest distillation—as the inner expression of *the essential itself*.

One could describe philosophy as a construction site; an immense *bildung* project shaping the structure where, instead of wood and hide and stone, we make a shelter out of the basic, but never simple, existential tragedies and felicities (or even plenitudes) of sense, of sensitivities, and finally, at the center of all this, our finitude. Following that imaging, we could comprehend and experience Steve Light's poems—which are succinct, short, deploying a precision of words; enunciations in which the association of utterance to meaning crosses the longest of distances yet is the most direct—as the refined and delicate edifice and interior of the essential that poetry always longs for, once the encumbering scaffolding of philosophy has been removed.

Poetry, perhaps, is consanguine with language itself, its gateway and origin even. It is where language comes closest to itself. But it is always just beyond language's grasp. For it is in the interstices of the word, the spaces that philosophy never succeeds in completely filling, that great poetry takes voice. And poetry, when it truly rises to itself, knows this, as will the reader, for that is precisely what it will have said. And that mastery of the word which we find in the poetry of Steve Light, where the building blocks of the complex are fashioned finally into a resonating and deeply felt immediacy at once simple and not so simple, is the hardest work of all.

It was Adorno who said that one must cross the frozen wasteland of the abstract to reach the concrete. Steve Light has traversed those ice fields, has indeed seen the frozen shores and glaciated peaks that only such a peregrination could endow and allow in order to reach what really matters, that which in a sense all of us know but ever and always forget, or even which life paradoxically makes us forget.

Saint-Just in the youthful prescience of an emerging world's dawn (as it could have been) noted that happiness was a new idea in the world. Steve Light in these duskier, wearier times brings us back, but wiser, wider, and more profound, to this core understanding, to this core of the real and the existential, to this core of *the most important*, so that it may emerge anew and resound in the deepest portions of ourselves.

—Joseph Gorlitzan, poet, critic, and translator

These gems illuminate the pathway out of the abyss. The intellectual rigor, the lyricism, the depth of feeling of these poems is an extraordinary achievement. The reader will find in this book a marvelous affirmation of life.

—Alan Silver, painter

Negativity, of course, is not absent from the poetry of Steve Light, however, it remains that an *affirmative breath*, an *optimism without naivety*, a profound assent to what is, always frees him from the negativist current of our modern conditions. It is a question for him, then, of a combat step by step, day after day, poem by poem. It is this trait that from the very beginning I have recognized as profoundly American in the noblest sense of the word. And this trait, all the stronger in him, means that the poetic DNA of Steve Light comes less from Poe, the most European of the great poets of the new world, than from Whitman, Pound, Carlos Williams, and Ginsberg. These are the poets who have had able recourse to a *lyrical positivity* that is forbidden all the great names of the modern European tradition. For me, personally, it is always this breath of fresh air, this right to innocence, obtained, of course, through difficult struggle, that I have always appreciated in these immense transatlantic poets. I find a similar "oxygenation" in the poems of Steve Light.

And, thereby, another distinct and striking trait of his poems: the spirit of the great European poets is omnipresent and is doubled by a concern no less unrelenting with the apocalyptic political events of the 20th Century, Auschwitz first of all. And, yet, this does not curtail or diminish what is the central and geneologically and philosophically very powerful sentiment of Steve Light: the human being, from her earliest Paleolithic beginnings, is the one who has *invented* happiness.

I must, in order to complete this brief presentation, accentuate another singularity of the poetry of Steve Light: it is what one could call, and in very close relationship with that about which I have previously spoken, a kind of *happy postmodernity*. And this is precisely and nothing other than the very real *historical thought* which is his. As all poetry dignified of the name, the poetry of Steve Light is a poetry of *intensity*; a poetry which in giving itself to thinking, seeing, and hearing, arrives finally at moving the soul to the point of tears.

—Mehdi Belhaj Kacem, philosopher and writer. Recent works include: *L'esprit du nihilisme: une ontologique de l'Histoire*; *Inesthetique et mimesis: Badiou, Lacoue-Labarthe et la question de l'art*; and *Algebra de la tragedie*. In addition, he is the translator of Dante's *La vita nuova* and Petrarch's *Trionfi*.

The Emergence Of Happiness

Steve Light

Spuyten Duyvil

New York City

Some of these poems previously appeared in *3 A.M., Hawai'i Pacific Review, Intranslation, Istanbul Review, La liberte de l'esprit, Los Angeles Review of Books, Rainbow Curve, Rattapallax, Vallum, Yefief,* and in French translation in *Europe* and in Italian translation in *Nuovi Argomenti*

© 2019 Steve Light

ISBN 978-1-949966-20-6

Cover art: Naoko Haruta, *Life #38: 'Music and Hours'* © Naoko Haruta, 2009

Library of Congress Cataloging-in-Publication Data

Names: Light, Steve, author.
Title: The emergence of happiness / Steve Light.
Description: New York City : Spuyten Duyvil, [2019]
Identifiers: LCCN 2019004166 | ISBN 9781949966206
Classification: LCC PS3612.I3447 A6 2019 | DDC 811/.6—dc23
LC record available at https://lccn.loc.gov/2019004166

for N

and

for my parents

CONTENTS

Somewhere In The Paleolithic	5
Aubade 1	6
Poem For Present And Future Generations	7
O, To Be Wind	8
Rimbaud	9
The Most Beautiful Image Of Our Century	10
Mimesis	11
Wanda Coleman	12
Aubade 2	13
Chopin: Nocturne #20 In C-Sharp Minor	14
I Get A Kick Out Of You	15
On The Sunny Side Of The Street	16
Alexander Pushkin	17
Bob Kaufman	18
Jardin Des Plantes	19
Poetry And Truth	20
Bud Powell: Tempus Fugit	21
Rhapsody On A Theme By Rachmaninov	22
The Beauties Of Poetry	23
Aubade 3	24
The Way You Look Tonight	25
Portrait Of An Artist	26
Aubade 4	27
Love Poem	28
On The Way From Athens To Venice	29
Love Poem	30
Aubade 5	31
Osip Mandelstam	32
Before The Mayans	33
Stéphane Mallarmé	34
In Search Of Lost Time	35
I Didn't Know What To Do	36
Quantum Gravity	41
Aubade 6	42
Nocturne 1	43
Preliminaries To An Aesthetic	44
Jean-Joseph Rabéarivelo	45

Marina Tsvetaeva	46
Don Juan And Jorge Luis Borges	47
Language And Painting	50
Nocturne 2	51
Ars Poetica	52
For My Father	53
Nocturne 3	54
Gwendolyn Brooks	55
Aubade 7	56
Lucretius	57
Amiri Baraka	58
Dinah Washington	59
Vladimir Mayakovsky	60
Mazurka 1	61
Ode To Joy	62
Nocturne 4	63
Anna Akhmatova	64
Nocturne 5	65
First Philosophy	66
Aimé Césaire	67
Nocturne 6	68
Nocturne 7	69
"Wstawać"!	70
Nocturne 8	71
Impromptu	72
Aubade 8	73
Aubade 9	74
December: Of Aphrodite	75
Ars Poetica	76
Helen And Aphrodite	77
Aubade 10	78
Aubade 11	79
Poetry And Mathematics	80
Easter Island	81
Aubade 12	82
Bergson And Einstein: A Haiku	83
Aubade 13	84
Vladimir Jankélévitch	85
On The Origin Of Language	86

Aubade 14	87
Aubade 15	88
Ballade 1	89
For All We Know	90
Nocturne 9	91
Nocturne 10	92
For The Mothers Of The Disappeared	93
Giacomo Leopardi	94
Nocturne 11	95
Love Poem	96
Aubade 16	97
Aubade 17	98
Ballade 2	99
Aubade 18	100
Luis De Gongora	101
Aubade 19	102
Against The Eternal Return Of The Same	103
Ever Of My Father	104
Constantine P. Cavafy	105
Nocturne 12	106
Evening Songs In Venice, Kyoto, And Dakar	107
Nocturne 13	108
"Dis Mois Connais-Tu L'Inconsolable?"	109
Nocturne 14	110
A Short History Of Painting	111
Aubade 20	112
Solidarities	113
Ballade 3	114
Nocturne 15	115
Sonnet To Eurydice	116
Aubade 21	117
Ballade 4	118
Love Poem	119
A Prelude To A Kiss	120
Aubade 22	121
Nike Of Samothrace	122
Aubade 23	123
Dancing In The Dark	124
Aubade 24	125

All The Things You Are	126
Paul Robeson	127
Migrations	128
Nocturne 16	129
Of The Perished And The Saved	130
Nocturne 17	131
Nocturne 18	132
Salvatore Quasimodo	133
Nocturne 19	134
Ode	135
Love Poem	136
Aubade 25	137
Mazurka 2	138
Audre Lorde	139
Ballade 5	140
Hart Crane	141
Variation On A Theme By Rachmaninov	142
Love Poem	143
Mazurka 3	144
Edmond Jabès	145
Aubade 26	146
Song For My Father	147
Mazurka 4	148
Aubade 27	149
Nocturne 20	150
Aubade 28	151
Of Konstantinos Kavafis	152
Like Someone In Love	153
Aubade 29	154
To Speak The Most Beautiful Language Of Our Century	155
On Happiness	156
Aubade 30	157
Aubade 31	158
Ever Of Gratitude And Happiness	159

The Emergence Of Happiness

SOMEWHERE IN THE PALEOLITHIC

After we abandoned the snows
And later the waters
We had painted on the walls
Of desert caves just beyond
The one remaining oasis

The rains enhanced our dreams
And each parting of the ways
Reduced the distance
Language instilled
In each migratory succession

We exclaimed the eagerness
Of the earth's rotation
Knowing that the arc
Of the comets would always
Return them to us
Knowing that the continents' drifts
Would one day fulfill
The rainforest's hunger
We had invented happiness

AUBADE 1

What is the language, the speech
Of the redwoods
In their circled formations,
In their meditations,
In their millenially enduring intimacies
And auditory depths and proximities?

As we walk among them
To speak even in whispers
Is already a breach
Is already to speak too loudly

POEM FOR PRESENT AND FUTURE GENERATIONS

> *"I dug Billie Holiday at fifteen,*
> *Wayne Shorter at twenty-five"*
> —Ray Bremser—

You should discover
Eric Dolphy and Booker Little when you are fifteen
You will love them intensely

They will help you to understand
Desire, the art of giving just weight to all things,
The impulse of the most beautiful of generosities

But you will not understand
Nor be able to feel intensely
The meaning, the notion,
The intricacy of the fact
That they died at thirty-six and twenty-three

Twenty years later you will love them more intensely
Not just because you will now understand
The meaning, the vibrato, the ache
Instilled in you by their deaths,
But because they will have helped you to understand
The encompassing vibrato of all affection itself

O, TO BE WIND

O, to be wind
Even when it is not yet
In flight

And so at ease
In its initial happiness,
Alert to this moment

When ever after
It can traverse
Every horizon
Without time

RIMBAUD

In memory of Yves Bonnefoy

Poetry never stops
Nor the felicities
And affections
Beneath the African distances
Assumed and awakened
By my anxious exuberance

THE MOST BEAUTIFUL IMAGE OF OUR CENTURY

Among all the snows of poets
Which would I choose?
And among all the rains of painters?
And what name should be given to the place where
Poetry and painting meet?

Certainly I know the weight, alas, of the rains
In Ernst's *Europe After the Rains*
But if the rains—and snows!—in Hiroshige and Hokusai
Cannot provide solace nonetheless
Ever do I think of them fondly

Poetry could well have preceded painting
But I imagine it did not
Yet if the comets preceded the oceans
And perhaps, wonderful paradox, even the oceans the rains
What of the mountains and rivers?

But when you told me that you used to
Ride your bike to school even on rainy days,
Holding your umbrella in one hand
And the steering column in the other,
I knew why painting precedes poetry
And why the most splendid answers
Can so fittingly precede the most splendid questions

MIMESIS

Stillness
Of the twigs

Their motionless
Language

Untranslatable
As the absence
Of birds

WANDA COLEMAN

In Memoriam

The fanciest colors weigh what?
The leaves will never say
And all the answers in one day
Will vanish will they not?

Weighs what the colors' fancy?
The letters of the words I've
Half forgot but always undergo, the sea
Tells different stories, or does it simply grieve?

Do colors rhyme?
How do they tell the time?
I'll find the unused answers

The gods remain bemused
But if we are enthused
Aren't we the nimbler dancers?

AUBADE 2

The wind goes
Round the world

Commencing
Where it ends

Like an unexpected kiss
On a windless morning

CHOPIN: NOCTURNE #20 IN C-SHARP MINOR:
VIOLIN TRANSCRIPTION BY NATHAN MILSTEIN

The longing
Of the piano
For the violin's
Interiors and intimacies,
Intimations and
Precipices…

I GET A KICK OUT OF YOU

—Ella and Bird!—

Poems do not come of their own accord
They are willed
Even there where the first words
Have emerged in the instantaneity
And vivacity of a mere turn of the head

*"When I'm out on a quiet street
And I suddenly turn and see your fabulous face!"*

Every poem would like to be the translation
Of that moment not even as fount
Of a subsequent congealment
But exactly as the face itself!

ON THE SUNNY SIDE OF THE STREET

It comes into view
These are the similitudes we weigh
In each and every commencement

That the *we* overcomes every asymptotic limit
While ever resounding as threshold desire

And yet the disjunction here is the unity
We find in every achievable joy

Life propels us
But these trees in yellow bloom
Always surprise us
Not even in their exultation
But in the loveliness of our own

ALEXANDER PUSHKIN

For Jean-Baptiste Para

This trace of blue
This broken glass
These notes, their hue
Unbend, undo, alas!

The day's missed cue
The chords' impasse
Light filters through
The nights amass

How blue the glass
And cold the sun's blue season
And weary weighs the sun

The simple subtle pass
The scale's scarce run
Scarce graze the note's *hélas!*

BOB KAUFMAN

My verse spirals and catches me up
In the eyes of its storms
And I know that I will always end up
Just there where the sentiment of my idea
Will have found the full affection
Of the most beautiful dance steps of each and every day

I carry with me so many special turns
To mark each and every moment in the glow
Of its prime-ultimate adventure
And if at any time it suits my fancy
I ascend to the exultant crests of North Beach's hills
To exclaim my verse to one and all and each

I know very well that every smile I encounter
Will appear again in what I compose
During all the enthusiasms
Of the sunsets and sunrises to follow come what may

JARDIN DES PLANTES
   (Botanical Gardens, Paris)

Reply to Emil Cioran

Music is an illusion?
But if each word were a song
And each river a dance?

Is the brilliance of the flowers
Merely their own dream,
The genial dream of an exultant memory

Or the magnificent paradise we carry,
Secret recompense, in the perpetual surprise
Renewed in each blinking of our eyes?

POETRY AND TRUTH

The sweetness
Of the most intense
Longing fulfilled
Is the asymptotic limit
Of the poem
Just as the poem
Is the asymptotic limit
Of the ceaseless
Longings of the sweetness
Of language itself

BUD POWELL: *TEMPUS FUGIT*

In memory of Andrew Hill

The sedulous storms cannot breach
Our counterpoints and crescendos

We swim the Hellespont
Knowing that trees don't die on sidewalks
And all the gods are useless,
Lacking opposable thumbs

In the downpours of the avid rains
We surrender neither virtuosity nor compass

RHAPSODY ON A THEME BY RACHMANINOV

In the extremity
Of what color
Was painting born?

But then what was the first
Question ever asked?
I love this thought:
How did the interrogative case arise?

Should poetry strive
To refrain from the interrogative form?
In philosophy it is too often
A form of coyness,
An unnecessary, an ineffectual litotes
But in poetry it is the light
Starting to break across the horizon
And in painting it is the light itself

THE BEAUTIES OF POETRY

Poets are not more inspired than others
They do not possess
A special faculty of longing
Which would enable words and music
To come to them
And they to music and words
In a reciprocal movement of
Resonance and recognition,
Hapax and happiness

Their gifts are mundane
They desire like everyone else
Although perhaps in a vibrato
Of slightly more duration

They speak like everyone else
If however they do no forget
To also speak of the *although*
And of the great surprise

They defend the smile
Against all the secrets of unhappiness

AUBADE 3

How much each of the continents'
Dawns differ and propel
Their mornings into still
More enchanting pleasures

And if the light of each diverges as do
The colors of sunset's antipodes

Yet even without having seen them all
We understand that every promise
Carries within it unknowingly
The convergence of its most ready fulfillment

THE WAY YOU LOOK TONIGHT

Across my hands
Memory has already
Entwined with every
Moment yet to come
So that it needn't ever
Search for that meeting point
In your gaze
Where I find
Everything I want to see

PORTRAIT OF AN ARTIST

The music of her paintings
Sounds and resounds within us
In melodies, harmonies, and crescendos
That we immediately realize
Are what the finest and sweetest point of our soul
Has ever and always longed for and desired

On dance floors and on boulevards,
On piazzas and on ocean sands
She honors Norma Miller and Ann Johnson
And Fayard and Harold Nicholas too!

She contests the hierarchies
But in the hierarchies of smiles her's is first,
And not only persuades
But also convinces *life*
That it too must exult!

AUBADE 4

I would like the metaphor
Of sailing to effortlessly
Bring forth poetic abundance

Winds, variances, sallies,
Are these to be the unencumbered arrival points
And ambulations, the tributes without tribulation
To generosities always already
Conveyed as spur, impulse, impassion?

Somewhere is the easiest of words
Never fatigued and never tiring or lagging in resonance
Or delight or in that leap
Which so soon as it has come to rest
Is once again propelled
Up and forth in flight and suspension

LOVE POEM

My lips
Upon the light

Upon the fathoms
Of your eyes

ON THE WAY FROM ATHENS TO VENICE

The train's momentum
Cannot outpace the clouds
Yet each day it rains

We set to imagining and even interpreting
The dreams of dolphins
But the dolphins just smile
Their dreams are happy ones

I suggest we write a film, *Against Vergil: A Happy Denouement*,
About Briseis' escape from Agamemnon and Achilles,
Her marriage to Aeneas, and the Greek departure
From Troy without their horses

You laugh and say that the dolphins
Have a much better idea
And suggest we extend tribute to them
In frolic and in dream
And proceed immediately to our berth

LOVE POEM

In the air
Where the world
Embraces

And all
Its sweetness
Trembles

AUBADE 5

The chromatic delights and intensities
Of the Appenines of Pasolini
And Moscow's Sparrow Hill
In the exuberances of Pasternak
Beckon and awaken my verse
In their scherzos and cascades

OSIP MANDELSTAM

All my hours fashion
This readiness
In syllables I pronounce
In every affinity I can find

I gather light from the sills
Resolute in its share
In the assembling dawn
Where seeds burgeon
Ever the more undaunted

BEFORE THE MAYANS

Where is this path?
But we were already
Overburdened with questions

Had we migrated or merely wandered?
We sought to rename the black and ochre
Stones strewn in meadows
We kept on till midnight
Through days and weeks

But mornings never satisfied
Our taste for noontide's beauties
Wading across streams,
Swimming against each river's current,
Above the plateaus
Orchards served as our compass,
The forests already red
In their autumn haste

The ruins we found did not perplex us
We knew there could never be a first arrival

STÉPHANE MALLARMÉ

What sunrise motes
Mingled in a star's
Gentle tears dance to notes
Glazed with the blackness of lacquers

What nostalgic eyes
Alert to every cue
Spread a rose hue
Over the morning sky's cries

Memories thicken into the dark
Estuaries of grief, a barque
Sinks into nothing

But this foam of words
Suffused in the sun's blue yearning
Upon the quickened retinas of weeping birds

IN SEARCH OF LOST TIME

If we could follow
A ray of light
Back to its origin
Back to its traversal
Across the thresholds
Not only of the recombinant moment
Of ready transparency
But of that infinitesimal
Distance light had crossed before
The expansion of the universe in cosmic inflation
Would we arrive at or even in this way possess or realize
Not merely what we call but rather again
What we feel in every affective depth?

I DIDN'T KNOW WHAT TO DO....

> *"...Consider if this is a man*
> *Who works in the mud*
> *Who does not know peace*
> *Who fights for a scrap of bread*
> *Who dies because of a yes or a no.*
> *Consider if this is a woman,*
> *Without hair and without a name*
> *With no more strength to remember,*
> *Her eyes empty..."*
> — Primo Levi—

Ever thereafter I would recount
The conclusion of Primo Levi's
Se questo e un uomo (If this is a man),
This conclusion of perfection

This perfect act of gratitude
That finds in such gentle and perfectly
Formed understatement
The perfect tone,
Sentiment, resonance

The Soviet army is approaching
("...Already for some months
Now the distant booming of the Russian guns
Had been heard at intervals...")
And the SS command has decided
To evacuate Auschwitz and
All its prisoners with the exception
Of the sick and dying

Levi reasons there will be greater
Peril on the forced march west
Than by remaining in the camp hospital

"All the healthy prisoners
(Except a few prudent ones
Who at the last moment undressed
And hid themselves in the hospital beds)
Left during the night of 18 January 1945.
They must have been about twenty thousand,
Coming from different camps.
Almost in their entirety [they died or were killed]
During the evacuation march: Alberto was among them
So we remained in our bunks,
Alone with our illnesses, and
With our inertia stronger than fear..."

Days pass but the Soviets have not arrived
"...We all said to each other that
The Russians would arrive soon, at once;
We all proclaimed it, we were all sure of it,
But at bottom nobody believed it.
Because one loses the habit of hoping in the *lager*
And even of believing in one's own reason...
With all relations broken already for eight days
With that ferocious world that still remained
A world, most of us were too exhausted even to wait..."

"...It was Somogyi's turn.
He was a Hungarian chemist, tall and taciturn.
Like the Dutchman he suffered
From typhus and scarlet fever.
He had not spoken for perhaps five days;
That day he opened his mouth
And said in a firm voice:
'I have a ration of bread under the sack.
Divide it among you three.
I shall not be eating any more...'"

On the 10th day, in the morning,
Somogyi dies

Levi and his French friend, Charles,
Carry the body out to the snow-covered yard
And as they deposit the body
They hear commotion
They look up and see Soviet soldiers
Peering into the courtyard

And Levi concludes his book:

"I didn't know what to do,
So I took off my hat."

Gratitude in its most exemplary manner,
Gratitude in its humblest and most generous forms,
Always overflows itself,
Overflows each and every
Attempt to express it

I had not looked at Levi's
Book for many years

I turned to the concluding page
To read those words
That by now I could easily
Have thought I had written myself:

"I didn't know what to do,
So I took off my hat"

But I did not find them
Or at least I did not
Find them in the form in which I had
Repeatedly recited, recounted them

"Charles took off his beret.
I regretted not having a beret."

I had transformed the words
And I had forgotten that these
Words did not conclude his book

"Charles took off his beret...."

Levi's concluding paragraph followed immediately:
"Of the eleven in the *Infektionsabteilung*
Somogyi was the only one to die in the ten days.
Sertelet, Cagnolati, Towarowski, Lakmaker and Dorget
Died some weeks later in the temporary
Russian hospital of Auschwitz.
In April, at Katowice, I met Schenck and
Alcalai in good health.
Arthur has reached his family happily
And Charles has taken up his teacher's profession again;
We have exchanged long letters and I hope to
See him again one day."

But there is another ending
Of beauty and perfection
And it is an ending produced neither by
Levi nor by me

I was recounting to N
That I had discovered that Levi's concluding words
Were not as I had remembered them

She said to me that the reasons
For my unconscious alteration
Of Levi's words were not as contingent
And unknowable as it might seem

She said in that exquisite
Form of generosity
That is always hers
That my alteration was a gift

Gift? It was the gift N
Gave to me:

"You felt bad for Levi,
You felt bad that he regretted
Not having a hat, and so
You gave him one!"

QUANTUM GRAVITY

What is the origin
Of the anxiety
Of the stones?

In light matter has seeded
The lure of duration
But must we then fall
There where the eye cannot rest
And the earth fears the call of its distance?

If the circle is but the emergence
Of grief in the impassive dimension of number
Then why does the light
Not bend to the rhythm of sadness?

AUBADE 6

Intensities of the stones
Beneath the afternoon sun
But the intensities of words
Is neither heat nor color
It is the part of them
We want to say the most

Poetry ever strives to reach this place
And the music that poetry always envies
Does so only at the cost
Of losing what words obtain
In all their recesses

How euphonious the sounds
Of the stones we send skimming
Across a river's expectant surface

NOCTURNE 1

Anguish fatigues me
In the cloudless hours
Of noon's retreat
There is no warning
Nor latitudes of commiseration

I swim too well to flail
But these distances are unaccustomed
To being traversed
I cannot restrain them
Nor encompass their certainties

Why does anguish feel so foreign
Even when its intimacies overwhelm me?
But the unavoidable answer
Only speaks of another crossroads, another chiasm
Because what is most precipitous
Is as lucid as is every tragedy penultimate

PRELIMINARIES TO AN AESTHETIC

These colors
Absorb music

Like music
Affections

And affections
The body

JEAN-JOSEPH RABÉARIVELO*

for Quincy Troupe

The distances are never quiet
While the labors of my days
Stand against this conjunction
I persist in contesting
With more than just a sum
Of afflictions and passions

Here the brevity of each storm
Is the sole chance I am given
In an endurance
Which knows every weight and measure
Of my anxious and accelerating vitality

I will not beseech the consequences
Amidst the long search which begins and ends
In a moment possessing the rhyme,
The murmur, the vastness of each and every telling

How stubborn transience in the mire and magnificence
Of lives I have inhabited
But which reach a limit in the vein
Of the token light I shall vanquish and annul

*—Madagascar poet, born 1901, died by suicide in 1937

MARINA TSVETAEVA

Told
In the sentience

Shivered
Inside

The wound
In resemblance

A chorus
Of stars

Exhaled
In each breath

DON JUAN AND JORGE LUIS BORGES

For a very long time
Don Juan has wanted
To construct a map
Of his desire
So that he will
No longer have to fear
Becoming lost in love

He enters a mapmaker's shop
And finds the mapmaker asleep amidst
Lengths of paper, rulers, drafting pens, and pencils,
But who, upon awakening
And upon hearing of Don Juan's dilemma,
Smiles broadly

Yet his reply is enigmatic:
"Only Borges can help you..."
"Borges? But you are a mapmaker
And he is only a purveyor
Of illusory figurations" responds Don Juan
"No, not illusory figurations, rather elliptical ones
And it is in the elliptical that you will find what you need"
Replies the mapmaker
"But where can I find your Borges?"
"Ah, that I do not know exactly
But I am in possession of a map
That might be able to help you"

Don Juan peruses it
But can only decipher
Arrows, lines, circles
Seeming to trace and then obscure pathways
From Barcelona to Shanghai,
Quito to Florence,

Venice to Kyoto,
Port of Spain to Amsterdam,
Buenos Aires to Paris, etc.

What is this?
He had not thought of Borges
As a world traveler—
Not even in figuration
And in any event surely the mapmaker must be wrong
He has no need of Borges
And for that matter
Why would he even need a mapmaker
When finally he really has no need for a map at all
Hitherto he has never been lost

He tosses the map away
Only to feel a tapping on his arm
And, turning, half expecting
To see Borges
As if fate in its ineluctable mischief
Would, as a rebuke if nothing else,
Surely have arranged

Yet the visage he sees
And the voice he hears,
"Senor did you lose this?"
Tells him that he is now
Surely lost, lost irretrievably

But Borges is beside himself
He has lost a character who is more than essential
It was from her that he has learned
All his narrative secrets—and poetic inventions

He rushes from street to street,
City to city, continent to continent to no avail
And then, weary and almost to the point
Of a valorous and chivalrous resignation—and admission,
He alights upon a mapmaker's shop

"A map, I must have a map
I've lost my central character!"
The mapmaker is at once startled, alarmed, bemused
How could Borges be in his shop?
The mapmaker rummages through heaps of scrolls,
Folders, cabinets, drawers, and then realizes his mistake
He has given the map
Which could have helped Borges
To Don Juan by mistake

What course to take now?
It's not so much his reputation which he must preserve,
Rather it is from a sense that the aleatory
Is always intractable
And that one's only strategy in defense
Must be to try and outbid it
He gives the map meant for Don Juan to Borges

But it is no use
She who had enchanted him
With her tales, her diction,
Her syntactic and narrative paradoxes and pirouettes,
Has run off, run off with Don Juan
Who now regales her, charms her
By reciting to her by memory stories, poems
By an Argentine author of whom she has never heard

LANGUAGE AND PAINTING

Build on each word a color
Build on each color a word
The sea in green
The sand in yellow
The sun in ochre
What if the first
Word ever spoken
Were *horizon*?

NOCTURNE 2

At the threshold
Of sense
We bruise
In the irrevocable
Breach

ARS POETICA

In memory of Alain Suied

Whether or not the poem
Shall overtake
Its mobile similarities
To whatever it is
It tries to name

I will not doubt
Its anxieties
Nor will I suspend
Its intricacies
Or append
Its sudden termination

FOR MY FATHER

In the first year
Of my father's death

I ate stars
And shivered in the sun

NOCTURNE 3

In your weariness can you remember
The weariness of the light, endless
In its distance, its travel, its irreversible eternity,
Its solitude, its destiny always without arrival?
But does the light remember us, does
It carry our weariness and our irreversible tragedies
Of which it too can be a portent?

GWENDOLYN BROOKS

We are lifted out
Into our own evocation
Spoken in our own lost language
As if another knew the one
Thing that no other could ever know
Wondered, wandered,
Scarcely whispered
Back to us alone

AUBADE 7

Does the universe need encouragement
Or do its galaxies suffice for commiseration?

I love these tender and consoling questions
And if the universe will always hide its answers
It is not out of stubbornness but merely from modesty
And in that we will always be in accord

LUCRETIUS

The fever
Of novae
In the hurtle
Of leaves

Velocities of munificence
In the fearless
Calm of the stones

AMIRI BARAKA

What breath
What source
Of brooding sense
Impassions and conveys
What daunting care
Illuminates the eyes' swift rise

What shuddered outcry
What amplitude of mind
What sharp and subtle discontent
Bestirs this brimming laughter,
Congealed uproar
In every sequence of these prescient feelings

Against what false duration strains
The mind's brave course
The wiser turn and salient tides

Against what portion of constraint prevails
The pith and pulse,
The soundings and the consequence
Of each and every promise kept and sung

DINAH WASHINGTON

Around the heart
The fervor
Each time
I'm through with love

Bells peeling in the strain
Of the outstretched affection

Or to change the tide
Of the registers
And densities of grief

And *time after time*
All the brave
Whispers along
All the keyboards

The rage of light
In the last breath
The rage of dying
In the living stream

VLADIMIR MAYAKOVSKY

Where are all the notes
Of all the songs
We dare to sing?

Love can always heal
Though migrant birds
Can lose their way

It's still a sign
The falling snow
And ever a respite
A shy delight
Restrained yet unrehearsed

MAZURKA 1

I will never know arctic rainbows
But the arctic is no more
Could one transcribe for the violin
The solitude of comets?

ODE TO JOY

In memory of Frank O'Hara

Joyous poems enfold me
If fate is always a tributary
Then language may well be too
The magnitudes of evolution
Are neither in drive nor reason nor affect
But accretion's mysteries are no more apparent
Than those of poetry and dance

Far back is not where poems begin
But they always seem to render the past
No matter the futurity of their promise

If I hurry today
And linger tomorrow
What will truly matter
Shall still know its share

What will it be like the day upon which
Calendars are no longer necessary?
And the joyful tenor of our answer
Is not diminished even on those days
When we miss the sunrise

NOCTURNE 4

What denouement
Curls inside each word
As it imparts
Its rhythm to the next?

Across what reach
Must it pass,
This marvel
And the adventure
Which sustain the elan
Of arduous commencement?

Every suggestion would
Be a riddle
Were it not already
An answer to a question
Too quick to be posed

Solace may yet elude the poem,
May yet elude us
But we know
As does every poem
That in this resides but
A lesser truth

ANNA AKHMATOVA

Where the sorrow
Of the blue
Distance absorbs

The languor and the light
And all this somber sweetness
An appetite of restless calm
Conveys our banished secrets

In a voice ranging in its share
The stemmed and starred clairvoyance

NOCTURNE 5

In what direction
Does anguish point?
If only it could be placed
Inside a compass
And the compass
Tossed out to sea

But would it sink
Or would it bob irrevocably
On the surface
From ocean to ocean,
Constant buoy
For us all?

FIRST PHILOSOPHY

Am I still inclined to polemics?
Surely I would like to reproach
The stars for their indifference
Yet black holes are as mysterious
To them as to us

Am I a narrator even if
Stories tell themselves
But poems do not?

Too often we forget
Not that what is far off was long ago
But that now its present is just like our present

Simultaneity is more resilient than paradoxical
And Bergson and Einstein can form a chiasm
Not of opposition
But of beneficence and charm

If the quantum world
And the world of relativity
Cannot be reconciled
Perhaps it is because complimentarity really is
The most abiding of all perceptions

AIMÉ CÉSAIRE

A sweep of woods
Where we run sand-bright
To the cliffs ever teeming

Torrent beds where the spiral-toned
Labor is won from the patience,
From the steadfast science of nets

Sculpt in the word affection's array
Scribe in the light the famished splendor
The munificent landscape traversed
Endeared in our panoramic and untethered ascents

NOCTURNE 6

If we are unsure
Of our anxieties
It is not because life is episodic
They are the surfeit
Of our mobile perceptions

If only time could
Just once know sorrow
But it never does
Being the elixir
Of our own

NOCTURNE 7

These sunsets before the storms
Are the reminders
Of lost occasions that eddy
In our dreams
And for which every smile
Strives valiantly, vainly
To be our solace

"WSTAWAĆ"! [Get up!]**

In Memory of Primo Levi

Do not sleep
Lie still
And never close
Your eyes
One blink
And dawn
Shall be upon you

**—*Command to awaken in Auschwitz. Immediately thereafter followed the "selections" as to who would live and who would die (See for example Primo Levi's poem, "Ad hora incerta" ["At an uncertain hour"] and the passages pertaining to "wstawać" in Levi's book* The Drowned and the Saved.

NOCTURNE 8

To the heart's bitter haste
Time never draws near
Having taken too much time
Darker in its lucent weight

We are rest and speed
Pneumatic and immutable scars
In the painless expanse

IMPROMPTU

A calamity of ships
In an umbrella of hills

Islands stacked
Upon islands
In tectonic rehearsal

And in every direction
The winds in irretrievable splendor
Convey their oceanic surprise

AUBADE 8

The spheres relent their mourning
Galaxies multiply in exuberant gaiety
They celebrate their Ptolemaic enchantments
Fearing not the dark energies of their mortality
But only that the horizon never ends

AUBADE 9

What could have been remembered
Was that sparkle in the leaves
Just before the last downpour
And the last of the dinosaurs
Washed away into the lakes and streams and crevasses

Could the impact of the meteor
Have been heard by every living creature
And if it could have been
What would that tell us
About the sparkle of the leaves
And the heralds and increasing multiplications
And chromatic delights of flowering plants?

DECEMBER: OF APHRODITE

for W.S. Merwin

One more poem
Before the year is through

It's not enough
To speak of tumults and tempests
Or of the sweetness
Dispersed throughout
All our embraces

And isn't the word
Magnificent lovelier still
Than all its rivals,
Majestic, marvelous, mellifluous...?

ARS POETICA

Months can go by
Where no poems come to me
However much I fervently seek them out
The days too short for my desires
Too long for my anguish and anxieties

But no sooner do
I pick up a volume of Pasolini
Then poetic desire
Unfurls so easily
In surfeit and sequence
In solace and surprise

HELEN AND APHRODITE

Aphrodite cannot find her mirror
She should know where to look
But she has fallen asleep
And feverishly dreams of running off with Paris
To the lands of the Iberians
Or better to the ever verdant highlands stretching south beyond
The last reaches of the great African desert,
That beyond which fills the dwellers of Olympus with wonder,
With longing, with the intensity of all their imperishable desires

Yet it is at this very moment that Helen has awakened,
Troy does not fall, Rome does not rise
The morning light shines
Upon all her nudity
Upon the serenity of her lips
Forming all the words of her delight and her resolve

Yes, Helen of Sparta has spurned the gods and Paris
There shall be no thousand ships
And leaning down to unclasp and remove her sandals
So as to walk through the incoming tide
She finds a mirror
But when she looks into it
She discovers it is transparent

She gazes out upon the waves, the expanse
And catching a glimpse of a dancer, a woman
She remembers from the court of Sheba,
A dancer now escaped and beckoning from the prow
Of a vessel whose sails are being hoisted,
She casts the mirror upon sands the tides cannot reach
And swims with ever more eager sensation
So as to reach the craft before the winds pick up and fill all its sails

AUBADE 10

Will there still be a banquet?
The lenses need polishing
But Spinoza has gone into exile

Why have these stories eluded us?
History is propelled
By contingencies which were lost not gained,
At least for those who think
History has a propulsion

You would think that history
Would itself grow weary
Of all that it has lost
But no rest for the weary
Is perhaps the most historical
Of all sage counsels
And in any case we learned long ago
That commencements elude
Everything save happiness itself

AUBADE 11

What does it carry away
The light that passes through us
On its way to the other side of the galaxy,
And then beyond to the other side
Of all visibility
And then beyond again?
And those that will receive it
At each and every juncture
In this endless skein
Of iridescence and irresistibility,
What will they add to it
In laughter and cheer,
Prescience and *prestissimo*?

POETRY AND MATHEMATICS

In reply to Alain Badiou

What does mathematics think of poetry?
And what does poetry think of mathematics?

But if the swallows at the end of their migration
Were to falter and turn back
To where would they return?

Mathematics is the perfect circle
That poetry can never know
But poetry never needs
To return anywhere,
Being always the perfect arrival

EASTER ISLAND

The distances still called to us
Forests gathered in our midst
Time could now exalt us
But we did not know, sadly,
That we would reduce it
To naught but our measure alone

Clambering up trees
We saw rivers
Receding upon their banks
And the stone foundations
We had forgotten
And the westward oceans
We had once crossed
But never named and which perhaps
We would never be able to name

AUBADE 12

But what shall be our arrival,
Circled in the distance,
That has won everything,
And these dances,
And the tenderness
Of light and laughter
In the marvels of our delight

BERGSON AND EINSTEIN: A HAIKU

For Elie During

Black Holes are in us,
Memory, around which we circle
Ever and ever faster

AUBADE 13

> *"...Autumn in New York..."*
> —Bird, Bud, Ella, Sarah—

The sorrow
Of the leaves
Of the trees
In their parting

Yet how tender
Is our joy
In autumn

VLADIMIR JANKÉLÉVITCH

In Memoriam

There is a voice
Glazing the wind with faint
Tints of quiet, a voice
Trailing the diaphanous restraint

Of the colors of silence,
A voice without taint
Lost in wordless grace
In a weightless leap, in a feint

ON THE ORIGIN OF LANGUAGE

As the poem starts it falters
Across deserts winds falter too
Or turn round
Yet failing in this
To return to their
Point of origin

Driving from Paris to Fontainebleau
I was stunned at how green it was, unending

How many of the world's languages
Have I never heard?
But they do not seem foreign to me
Nor mysterious in any way

It is the Paleolithic languages
About which I wonder
And which do seem
In their disappearance
To contain the most intimations of all

But that is not their dilemma
It is that the winds
Have never had
A point of origin

AUBADE 14

Destiny and delight
Are not always opposed

I don't want
To misjudge their fervor
But I wearied
Of equations long ago

Mandelstam spoke
Of the yeast of the earth

I would like to say
That ever is it so
Only so that we—and he!—
May know the fruits
Of every beautiful fancy and fate

AUBADE 15

At the sight-lines of our renderings
These enamored pictures
Of the sallies of joy

This charm that we feel upon awakening
Sweet lassitude and the pleasure of boundlessness
And ever their graceful and gracious combinations

So close are we to these conjugations
That a marvelous fleetness gives rise
To our most immediate rhythms
In which our resonant anticipations
Overcome every distance
Between spirit and sense

BALLADE 1

And then the weary turn
And ever in resemblance
The famished disillusion of the eyes' stern art

Yet in the dance
And in the blooming
Pleasure of the brief recess

The glance so bright
As if a summons and a cry
The rounding measure in the harbor's temperate lore
And winds bestir the calm of voyages rehearsed

Causeways in the open
Roar and in the gasp
And span from every shore
Tempests of a clement scale
The stars in gleaming foam
Fervid embrace which time alone defends

FOR ALL WE KNOW

"...we may never meet again..."

—Dinah Washington, Nina Simone, Abbey Lincoln...—

Just there where the coastal trees
Entwined with the arriving light
The stones' polished merriment enthralling us
We began to sing

I could have said
The cliffs will surely hold
And exultant in lucent waters
We swam for the remaining shore

Could we have borne
The strength, the surplus
Of our affections,
Slipped through the waters
As if guided
By a faultless song?

We knew what we had found,
What the weathers so generously gave us
And later, on starred sands,
We knew we had won much more than just the day

NOCTURNE 9

There is a fatigue,
A grief, an anguish,
Which the leaves are unable to absorb
Into one last color,
Into one last span,
One last season

And the rains shall neither compel
Nor compose these lost
Occasions, nor shall my
Repetitions transcribe and redeem
A lost inducement,
A botched, a banished claim

NOCTURNE 10

The world aches
In the extremity
Of light borne by each eye
In its vastness

Yet it does not veer
From its contingent,
Its recalcitrant course

Leaving the light
In all our eyes
To bear the debt
Of every grief unconsoled

FOR THE MOTHERS OF THE DISAPPEARED

"I always think [she/he] will return,
Always, whenever I see someone coming
towards me..."

And each
And every one
Fashioned in her eyes

And song birds drift
In the clear
And in the light

GIACOMO LEOPARDI

Between regret and death
It is not the ever more
Silent and expansive
Void which I must pass through
But rather the ever
More dense and claustrophobic duration

NOCTURNE 11

And life and world without wind?
And when the ice had melted,
The polar caps reduced to filaments
The winds could no longer
Feign their indifference,
Could no longer resist their protest
They ceased completely

LOVE POEM

I am propelled
In these forays
Where days
Enfold our serenities
And I breath your desire

AUBADE 16

You were wearing yellow
And in the simultaneity
Of your smile and my anticipation
I knew all the more that color originates
In this pleasure taken
From that which we desire to see the most

I would have liked
To have found in one single aphorism—
Light is the mythology of color
And color is the mythology of light—
The kind of happiness that knows that
Origin can never be the goal

But I knew that you had already thought of that
And I marveled at all the things
And all the worlds that
Offered up their explanations to you
As both their gift and their gratitude

AUBADE 17

There is no image
To depict
An absence
Of leaves

You would have
Fallen in the snow
But I caught you

I had forgotten
That the deserts
Beckoned us

I cannot recall
What made us forget
To turn back

A mirage would have shielded us,
Would have given us comfort,
But we reached the ocean instead

BALLADE 2

Reached in the glare
In the tide turning
Where light whirls
In abandoned harmony
In the wake of this need
In the tempest's dense maze

And the strains stirred
In the broken thread
And the stumbling tread

Mazed voice in the desperate presence
To seed in forgotten narration
Instilled in the sudden agon of eye and of heart

A chorus to mime
To the dip of each sail
In a language deciphered no more

Each morning evinces the fate
In the vein of each sorrow

AUBADE 18

The impending fragrance of meadows
In all their exuberant gifts

And a colloquy of anticipations
In their sudden insistence
Where every enactment
Shall be gathered

LUIS DE GONGORA

Sun to swiftest looming, borne
Amidst the fated
Rushes, shorn
To every martyred season, hurried,

To every stress and form and reason, torn
From yearning light, from root and reed
The word-fled promise sworn
To vest the spark, the sum, in need

And nest, the spoken turned
Within the word-imbrued
Fortune against the tragic sacrifice

The ferment
Of the unthrown dice,
The *never-done* besieged within each torment

AUBADE 19

Where sweeps these tides
Of fervor ever festive
When all I could want
Eddies in the early morning
Commencement and commiseration?

AGAINST THE ETERNAL RETURN OF THE SAME

If destiny is not
Just a color
But a panoply of light

Then the arc
Of every life
Is a momentum accelerated

Upon the beneficence
Of every horizon's
Lassitude and generosity

EVER OF MY FATHER

Not once, never
Did I experience
A moment, an instance
A circumstance
When or where you acted or
Even thought to act
In a selfish way

CONSTANTINE P. CAVAFY

Unstilled the calm
The still and somber span
The delicate and tender skein
The blameless winds arouse

The patient breath
In brim and bloom
The will to joy ever suspires

NOCTURNE 12

We need rain
But the horizon
Is too insistent

Has a species
Ever perished
In anything other than silence?

But how voluble
Is the mind
In the presence of flowers

What were
The last words
Of Homo Erectus?

EVENING SONGS IN VENICE, KYOTO, AND DAKAR

And then cities sparkling
Even more than beneath
Their own noonday suns
And even more serene
Than beneath twilights and evenings
Where the wind is an invocation
And the dark the loveliest kind of recompense

NOCTURNE 13

And if there were *just once*
One time for these words
And yet ever must they be repeated
In and out of whatever sequence assails us
And never just once

Is this where we might
Find the language of tribulation
And a language no longer
Weighted beneath an impossible exit?

"DIS MOIS CONNAIS-TU L'INCONSOLABLE?"
(Tell me, do you know the inconsolable ?)
　　—*Charles Baudelaire*—

I have long tried to keep
The inconsolable out of reach
But the inconsolable does not know any distance
It is that part of us
Which is the most intimate of all
And if finally we cannot hide from it
It is because it always stays hidden
Until it is too late to evade its grasp

NOCTURNE 14

Which words repeat
The rhythm and joys of life?

Unhappy memory
Spendthrift and sure

In which years
Did the swallows
Return without regret?

A SHORT HISTORY OF PAINTING

The trapezoidal mania of consciousness
Erecting its cylindrical pain
And somewhere between the
Real and the symbolic
We imagine what we could never dream

AUBADE 20

The day was to have begun
Stories came to me
All the weathers contributed in narration

But to what end
I cannot yet say
Mystery is its own province

Do not long for the day
Nor wish that the day
Would long for you
Rather and above all have longing
Long for you

SOLIDARITIES

Songs yearn amidst
The chalk and dust
Of shattered bricks

A tattered curtain hangs
In the air, caught on a windowless ledge,
Pennon of wind and wherefore

An undaunted child wears
The burden of time and suffering
On her tiny stretch of shoulders

And through a voice,
As through an hourglass,
A torrent and an endless rain

BALLADE 3

A scarce movement of lips
Where a wound endures
Like the thirst of the sand
When a desert wind dies
Like memories yearning
On the surface of eyes
Like the moans of a swan
Giving birth in the dark
Like the courage of trees
All alone in their bark

NOCTURNE 15

And if this grief shall not relent
Nor the knowledge of its origins
Nor in any redeeming turn
That could ever be gathered
And every paradox and even this one
Is neither ready nor sufficient
In the days which swirl through gaze and gamut

SONNET TO EURYDICE

But yet to sail
Through summer's swift event
The ash-green distance spent
The subtle wail

The frantic weather
Raises from the scree
The wind in all its gravity
Undone the tether

Of the soaring flight
Flowers amidst the anxious site
Their transient tales which hold the calm

Mimetic anguish of each sudden storm
Image and a tracing form
Impassioned in quick semblance of divine alarm

AUBADE 21

Flowering plants are so recent
Emerging perhaps as little
As 140 million years ago

I never thought of this before:
I do not know the names
Of any green flowers

I've always preferred gardenias to roses
But when Pasolini spoke of walking
Coatless in the jasmine wind
I knew that he had found
The perfect promise,
Precedent, commencement

BALLADE 4

And then in that pause,
Enduring wonder and affection,
Watch, if the branches
Shall yield their weight
In the instant of their desperate summons
Or if the gentlest ones shall meet and celebrate

Herald, of noon and its lost tides,
Promise to the hope-wracked,
The teeming splendor of our vertiginous aspect,
Duration of a bell which we, exultant,
Shall always refuse to toll

LOVE POEM

On your transparent lips
How much these words gleam

A PRELUDE TO A KISS

> *"...l'eternidad de un beso victorioso!"*
>
> —*Pablo Neruda*—

I need not add
To the poem's destiny
Nor to our's
This thought
Of a sudden expectation,
Too sweet to endure persists

AUBADE 22

How salient these tides
And their commencements
Beneath so many moons

Look for the sails
And the sounds
Of every magnificence

That will be our
Celebration, our key

NIKE OF SAMOTHRACE

Of course it is her wings
The wind, the world widening wherever she might go
And yet it is also in the euphonies of this word, Samothrace
Where we ourselves are propelled
In a wonder, a marvel, a joy
In a leap which we ever and always imagine
In a leap which we have always known could be ours

AUBADE 23

At a moment
When winters hesitate
In reveries we enjoin
With ready savor
Life pulses amidst landscapes
We had always foreseen
In splendors and serenities
That have but to choose
Their fancies and their musics

DANCING IN THE DARK

And to gaze into the eyes
Of someone who truly knows
And who knows also the roses and the crescendos
And the verve and vivacity
And also the ache,
But also the ardor
All the way from the Bronx, Poe Park, and Harlem
To Central, to Compton, to Long Beach Avenues

Yes, here are the roses, and here we dance,
The dance of every shadow and every light
And every broken breath
Mended and respired again
Into a new song,
Into a new dance,
Proximate, plentiful,
The dance, first and last,
Prime-ultimate and ultimate,
The dance always saved,
Last, exalted, jubilant!

AUBADE 24

You run so quickly
And I am waiting on the hillside
Even more joyous than had we rested in the brief spell
When the rains came and went
And we arrive in our embrace
And what we know and what has transpired
Are in the music that we are
And in the harmonies that are realized not just
In their encores but in our own as well

ALL THE THINGS YOU ARE

You do everything so well
It gives me the sweetest assurance
That I can tell you
In a manner more graceful
Than I ever could have before
That you are ever the more graceful,
The most graceful of all

PAUL ROBESON

And the sudden quickening
Through the length and longing

Open upon the light,
The verve, the vigor, the vivacity
Of stubborn hope

And sing
Justly
Sing

MIGRATIONS

for Gary Snyder

Faint aroma of tea, cinnamon,
And the artisanal tracings of bees

All the surfaces of memory,
All the articulations
Which speak in the clothing
Of moons, tides, blue weathers

Where the curling lines
Of the day's sequences
Form the transparent colors of quiet
The slender calls of dusk
Where herons move their flocks

NOCTURNE 16

Do truths know how to wait
Or is their legerity the sign
Of their most ardent desire
To unburden themselves
Of their too often hermetic fate?

Yet it is from them that we learn
Not only what it would mean to truly wait,
But also why they too know the inconsolable
In every rejuvenation they might think to undertake

OF THE PERISHED AND OF THE SAVED

What images return
In the mirrors of your hands?

You hold the light
Of vanished stars

Where pass your gently moving eyes
Upon all the surfaces of grief

NOCTURNE 17

In what expanse or region
Of the wind's swift wound
Do we restore the timbre
Of our humble calm,
The temper of our dance and leap?

NOCTURNE 18

There is sorrow
In this sudden rainbow
As if commiseration
Were its first
And ever present affection
Or even the eternal raison d'être
Of color and light

SALVATORE QUASIMODO

I slumber
In serene waters

A lunar peace
Imbues the heart of words

I slumber
In the equinox
Of sadness

Shiver
In the loneliness
Of words

NOCTURNE 19

A piece of paper rustles
And I jump to the heavens
The booksellers on the Seine
Have raised their prices
But on this August evening it rains
They are closed

Does Paris rejoice these
Summer chills and this
Northern wind which carries
But one last hope?

These evenings will not
Abandon their light so easily
And each peregrination marks
The sanguine rhythm
Of this perpetual dance
But I know that soon
I shall need a winter coat

ODE

*In memory of Vladimir Jankélévitch
and Lucienne Jankélévitch*

Against the plaque the flowers will rust
And no one will come to take them away

Is it a sudden light rain
Or a mere rustling of memory?

*né en 1922...
né en 1926...
né en 1903...
fusillé en 1944...**

Was it all simply my own dream?
Asks a brave and steadfast sage
Quelque part dans l'inachevé

Somewhere in the incomplete
Somewhere in the immense
Unaccompaniement

*—*Memorial plaques in Paris streets for those who 'fell for France'
during the August 1944 uprising of the Resistance during WWII*

LOVE POEM

I am weighted
Beneath
My longing

Like the sun
Beneath
Its light

AUBADE 25

Meander so gently
The breeze will not delay
Its episodic surmise
Nor its scansion
Nor the gamut of surprise

MAZURKA 2

We had never known each other
Beyond the ambience of my inclination and your smile
Or was it your inclination and my smile?

There is a sweeter rhythm in that
And even more the sympathy
The irreversible must always grant us
In its implacable will

What was there you gathered
In a composition whose libretto
You always imagined we would write

Somewhere across what could be
The shortest circumference
No matter the temporal
Lengths or distillations
If our smiles were to meet
Then we would know that
Sequence never abandons
The music it always holds in store

AUDRE LOURDE

Epigrams of light
Sound the transparence
The lucent and unblemished breezes
The churl and charge
The waves in all their flight

Epigrams of light
Colors wrought
From tender glass
From joy and resolution
Gathered in the gulls' unfettered sights

BALLADE 5

To wrest it simply
Sympathy's interior
Movement, motion, ache

The courage
Of every sympathetic grief,

And its symphonic infinity
Interlaced in every recollection

HART CRANE

The dip and pivot in the lithe
Coil of the wind
Seascape in the serene
Teeming of the heart
And the candor
Of the span and sequence
The distance in the eye's sage art

And now the arch and buttress
Of its weathered yearning,
The gusts and gamuts
Of the mortal pulse
And all the prescient stories
Unfurling in our guise

The storied constellation,
The calm surmise the windy
Summits gather from their quest
The simplest trace and greatest share
As if the storm's profusion
Sounds the greater care
The crush of humid air
A leap into the brave pneumatic glare

VARIATION ON A THEME BY RACHMANINOV

The blue-white winter sun whitens
In the blue of the ice
In the sparkle and hue
Of the bright white branches

And the shimmering bark
And the shivering sap
In the white night
Of the valiant and whispering leaves

LOVE POEM

Desire for you
In the staccato light

In hands full of ardor
And anguish

MAZURKA 3

Surprise in me
The gentle chime
Of dusky waters
A gaze exhaled
In sweet winds and swells

Surprise in me
The aftermath
Of the tides
Blameless rhythm
And the day's
Serene and gentle ascent

Surprise in me
The vast surmise
And the wandering song
Of love's open site

EDMOND JABÈS

In Memoriam

No pain inside the word
Nor in reason nor in rhyme
But then where is the word's pain?

No memory inside the word
Nor in breath nor in light
But then where is the word's remembrance?

No odyssey inside the word
Nor in distance nor in death
But then where is the word's birth?

AUBADE 26

In memory of Arlette Jabès

Islands sail above the horizons
As if in a universe without portents

Where rivers discern their desires
And the tides their ample abandon

Perhaps this was how serenity was born
And all of dawn's revels and gifts

SONG FOR MY FATHER

Even as a child I already carried the idea
Which was ever the more an inner pulse of gratitude,
A vivifying and encompassing warmth
And it arises now, stronger, more urgent with your passing
Each time I hear or take to singing
Songs which you would sing,
Sing for us, in celebration and as gift,
I'm in the Mood for Love, Summertime,
What a Difference a Day Makes,
Sentimental Journey, Manhattan...
And so on and so forth
In this panoply which envelops me
And ever will I see you, hear you, not just in voice
But in the splendor of knowing
That among all your gifts and sweetness
And all the gifts you so sweetly gave to us
You understood, you knew so intimately and tenderly
How to give to us the kind of delight
That would ever and always be the *embrace* of our feelings

MAZURKA 4

If we lose these days
To their reciprocal despairs
To our own reciprocal despairs
And the asymmetrical anguish
Which does not turn round
Yet we know that these days
And their reciprocities are ever ours
And the hours where what shall be
Need not be a crossroads
But a companion in song
Which outstrips all musing
And where memory too can sing

AUBADE 27

Swiftly in the mellifluous chime
You are waiting
Beneath the blue breeze

Speak to me then of your art
Of the graceful revels
That ascend the wind
In adumbration and allure

NOCTURNE 20

No divergence between these sentiments
And the most absorbent of colors

I am the privileged interlocutor of so many
But despair of the transience
Of each and every resonating word

There is grief
Which sinks into us
And there is grief
Into which we sink

And every truth
Must be twice told
And twice learned
And yet the truth
Of that resides in its instantaneity
And in every smile
That elicits one in return

AUBADE 28

Yes certainly the earth can feel us
In every instance of the utter exuberance
In these rare moments
When a breath absorbed in all its happiness
Pervades us so that we can feel the earth feel us
If we have the great fortune of that special existence
In which the horizon appears to us
With that expectation we feel ever in our youth
And which we will later realize is the most
Exalted way of being splendidly alive

OF KONSTANTINOS KAVAFIS

"Not without favor..."
He knows that he has often
Used the litotes,
At times without hesitation,
At other times only after considerable perplexity

He is not sure what
Has brought him to a halt at this moment
He remembers the length of time it took him
When he sat trying to decide
Whether to give to his Cappadocian poet, Phernasis--
Fashioner of an epic whose composition
Was interrupted by the outbreak of war with the Romans--
Use of this figure, this form

"Not without favor..."
Halt? He is certain that
This is the right, even the perfect
Phrase for the moment,
But to whom is it best suited
And even more of what kind
Of moment is it really a question?

Are all his verses, his lines
Answers to these musings,
These lapses, these halts, caesuras?

"Not without favor...."
The resonance of the phrase,
How much it vibrates within him,
And how much the sentiment of the idea,
Of its music transpires and precedes
And ever thereafter always lingers
As every poetic *favor*,
Every poetic *fancy*

LIKE SOMEONE IN LOVE

> *"...Lately I walk as if I had wings...*
> *gazing at stars, hearing guitars...*
> *like someone in love..."*
>
> —*Sarah Vaughan*—

To walk
Where the streets
Unfold in their ecstatic sweetness

Where every anticipation
Ever given
In a name
In a face

Where every step
Every turn
Every dance
And leap

As in a music
Resplendent in every
Note and recommencement

As in all
The vistas
In the bounding light

AUBADE 29

To say something
So precisely
That it passes
Even through itself
To a place
Of impossible misunderstanding,
So precise
That every color
Emerges as if
For the very first time

TO SPEAK THE MOST BEAUTIFUL LANGUAGE OF OUR CENTURY

If I say nothing at this moment
A moment that will have been
For me as splendid
A sequence of time
As can be gathered
In any foresight

How beautiful these interludes
Before and after every duration

It was you who spoke first
And for an instant that sustained itself
Far longer than I thought any smile
Propelled by such magnificence could last
I wondered if this were the most beautiful
Eloquence that could ever be possible

ON HAPPINESS

Ever the sensual shiver in this
In the earliest portion of the morning,
The little table with its scattered books
And the writing notebooks with their soft, textured paper
You had obtained for me in Florence and Nara
Your arms thrown round me
As you read over my shoulder
The words in their blackest of inks
Seeping into the page
The shades thrown open
And the sunlight
In every portion of the room,
As if that large and splendid window
Had gathered up for us
All of summer's solstice

AUBADE 30

Across the meadows
It might seem the redwoods
Beckon us to dally
Amidst the exalted truth of morning winds
And they do
This is their homage to the time
They have been given
And to us if in this quietness
We are able to partake of a generosity that
Is ever and all the most magnificent

AUBADE 31

I slip from I to we so easily
I reach for the branches
Dazzled by the yellow leaves

What colors will you choose
To paint this meeting
Of the brisk air
Delighted always
By its own plenitude
With the rustling of leaves
Which return every caress
Every whispered entreaty

EVER OF GRATITUDE AND HAPPINESS

When my father would speak on the phone
He would always doodle
In ever more baroque sequences
His energies bounding
Upon whatever might be at hand
Book margin, magazine, newspaper,
And no sooner was he done with his conversation
And had put the receiver back in place
My brother and I would rush with anticipation
To view these etchings always scintillating
And which he in complete
Insouciance—because he was
Seemingly unaware of anything
Other than the conversation in which he was engaged—
Would leave for us as one more gift
Of his unending generosity and care

Steve Light is a poet and philosopher. His most recent book is *Against Middle Passages* (New York: Spuyten Duyvil, 2017). He is the translator of Jean Grenier's *Islands: Lyrical Essays* (Los Angeles: Green Integer, 2005) and his writings and translations have appeared in many countries.

www.ingramcontent.com/pod-product-compliance
Lightning Source LLC
Chambersburg PA
CBHW012100090526
44592CB00017B/2638